TALK ABOUT
Internet Crime

Sarah Levete

WAYLAND

First published in 2009 by Wayland

Copyright © Wayland 2009

Wayland
338 Euston Road
London NW1 3BH

Wayland Australia
Level 17/207 Kent Street
Sydney, NSW 2000

Produced for Wayland by Calcium

Editors: Sarah Eason and Robyn Hardyman
Editor for Wayland: Katie Powell
Consultant: Jayne Wright
Designers: Paul Myerscough and Rob Norridge
Picture researcher: Maria Joannou

British Library Cataloguing in Publication Data:
Levete, Sarah.
   Talk about Internet crime.
   1. Computer crimes—Juvenile literature.
   I. Title II. Internet crime
   364.1'68-dc22

ISBN: 978 0 7502 5736 7

Printed in Malaysia

Wayland is a division of Hachette Children's Books, an Hachette UK Company
www.hachette.co.uk

The majority of situations in this publication are fictitious and are posed by models.
Any resemblance to real persons, living or dead, is purely coincidental.

The website addresses (URLs) included in this book were valid at the time of going to press.
However, because of the nature of the Internet, it is possible that some addresses may have
changed, or sites may have changed or closed down since publication. While the author and
Publisher regret any inconvenience this may cause the readers, no responsibility for any
such changes can be accepted by either the author or the Publisher.

Every attempt has been made to clear copyright. Should there be any inadvertent omission
please apply to the publisher for rectification.

Picture acknowledgments: The author and publisher would like to thank the following
for allowing their pictures to be reproduced in this publication:
Cover photograph: Shutterstock/Killroy Productions.
Interior photographs: Corbis: Dex Images 40, Ron Sachs/CNP/Sygma 14–15, The Stocktrek
Corp/Brand X 38–39, Martial Trezzini/EPA 6; Dreamstime: Dmitriy Yakovlev 22; Fotolia:
Mikhail Lavrenov 7; Istockphoto: Jaimie Duplass 34, Rich Legg 5, Cliff Parnell 26, Andreas
Reh 42, Nicole S. Young 16; Rex Features: 9, David Hurrell 24; Shutterstock: Andresr 36, Yuri
Arcurs 1, 27, 28, 44, 47, Noam Armonn 35, Beaucroft 12, Nikki Bidgood 31, Ana Blazic 8, 23,
William Casey 13, David Davis 17, 30, Rafael Franceschini 20–21, Miodrag Gajic 4, Alexander
Gitlits 29, Johanna Goodyear 10, Ramzi Hachicho 18, Christopher Halloran throughout,
Damir Karan 2–3, Marina Krasnorutskaya 37, Magicinfoto 32–33, Mika Makkonen 19, Monkey
Business Images 41, Losevsky Pavel 25, Andy Piatt 43; Wayland Archive: 47.

CONTENTS

Chapter 1

What is Internet crime?

How often do you use the Internet? Every day or once a week? Do you use it at school or at home? The Internet is a vast source of information. It can be educational, provide a way to chat to friends and be a place to play games. But some people use the Internet for criminal purposes, such as stealing from online bank accounts and identity fraud.

Crime and the Internet

Cybercrime, e-crime and hi-tech crime – these are just some of the terms used to describe crime which is carried out through the Internet. This fast-growing area of criminal activity is an increasingly difficult problem for security organizations and the police.

Most people associate the Internet with fun, not crime. Being aware of its risks keeps you safe online.

From harassing an individual via his or her computer, to using someone else's personal details to get hold of their money, criminals have taken advantage of the ways in which people now use the Internet to shop, chat and play. Internet crime includes:

- Fraud or cheating.
- Stealing or misusing personal information.
- Deliberately destroying computer software from computer to computer.
- Bullying.

Sending abusive messages to computers or mobile phones via the Internet is nasty and distressing, and in many cases it is a crime.

Some Internet crime is carried out by individuals working alone, other cybercrimes are carried out by groups of people who work together in criminal networks. These groups use the Internet to communicate with each other and organize their criminal activities.

What's the harm?

Some people think that cybercrime is less serious than crime that involves people directly, such as stealing a purse or bullying with fists. But Internet crime doesn't just harm computers – they are only the tools used to carry out the crime. The crime affects the life of the victim who is using the computer at the other end.

A global problem

The Internet crosses international borders. There is no single international organization which monitors activity on the Internet. Laws about what activity on the Internet is legal or illegal vary from country to country. The law also depends on where the crime takes place. For example, the British police may be unable to take action over Internet fraud carried out on a computer in China.

FACTS

These figures show the percentage of the population in different regions who used the Internet in 2008. They also show how much Internet use has increased in eight years. As Internet use increases, so too does Internet crime.

Country	Percentage of population	Internet use percentage growth 2000–2008
Africa	5.3	1,031.2
Asia	15.3	406.1
Europe	48.1	266.0
Middle East	21.3	1,176.8
North America	73.6	129.6
Latin America/Caribbean	24.1	669.3
Oceania/Australia	59.5	165.1

Source: www.internetworldstats.com

A brief history of the Internet

The Internet is a network of billions of computers around the world. It began as a research project carried out for the United States Department of Defense in the early 1960s. The project was looking into ways to link up different military and university departments. It was then called ARPA (Advanced Research Projects Agency) and then later APRANET. By the 1970s the linking of the computers used within some university departments, governments or organizations, was known as the Internet.

In 1989, Tim Berners-Lee and Robert Cailliau invented the World Wide Web, a system of interlinked documents accessed via the Internet.

Over the next twenty years, the Internet grew rapidly until it was used by millions of people around the world. The World Wide Web, or web, is made up of millions of 'pages' and is one way of accessing and sharing information across the Internet. Other ways include email and instant messaging. Today, you can send as much information as is contained in a 10-volume encyclopaedia, from one computer to another, with just the click of a mouse.

Who owns the Internet?

The simple answer is no one and everyone. Internet service providers (ISPs) allow you to access information on the Internet. ISPs have guidelines about what material they allow, but they are not directly responsible for the content of the millions of websites viewed through their service.

The age of technology

You may have shown an adult how to use the Internet or sorted out a computer problem for them. Young people are often more skilled at programming and computer use than their parents or carers who weren't born in the age of technology and taught computer skills. As a result, many adults are not aware of the possible dangers of the Internet and how young people especially are at risk from Internet crime.

Children are usually more computer literate than their parents. Adults often don't know how young people use the Internet to chat and message; nor do they know the risks.

FACTS

How often do children use the Internet?

✻ **99% of children in the United Kingdom have access to the Internet.**

✻ **90% of children in the United Kingdom have a computer at home.**

✻ **89% of young people (aged 12–17) use the Internet at home.**

✻ **77% use it at school.**

✻ **60% use it in the library.**

Chapter 2

Spying, stealing and vandalizing

Many people are skilled and confident users of computers. They know how to instal and even program computers and they are good at trouble-shooting when something goes wrong. But some people use these skills to cause deliberate harm to the software and to gain information from other people's computers. This is called hacking.

What is a hacker?

The word hacker was first used in a positive way to describe someone's skills as a talented computer programmer. Today it is used negatively, to describe 'breaking into' someone else's computer to cause harm. The term cracker is also used to describe this. Hackers can send out unpleasant and untruthful information, steal someone's personal identity, and send out programs, called computer viruses, which deliberately destroy and alter information. This is online vandalism.

Some people think hacking into a friend's computer is a joke, but it is very distressing for the victim.

In the media

At the age of 16, Jonathon James was sent to prison for six months. James had hacked into major computer systems in the American Department of Defense. This department was responsible for reducing the threat to the United States from nuclear and other weapons. James managed to crack the code to the department's complex computer system, and gain access to private emails and employees' usernames and passwords. James also cracked into the computers of NASA (the North American Space Agency). As a result, NASA had to shut down its computer systems for a while.

Why do people hack?

The effects of hacking range from the irritating to the devastating. Some hackers cause inconvenience; others cause serious harm to organizations and individuals. The motives are often unclear. For some people, hacking starts off as an innocent challenge to test their programming skills. However, showing off programming skills becomes illegal if it involves tapping into someone else's information, altering or destroying it. Some people claim that they hack into computers to show how easy it is to gain access to confidential information, especially in large government organizations.

The United States government believes that Gary McKinnon, a British man, hacked into classified information in its military and government computers to threaten the security of the country. However, Gary McKinnon claims he is a 'bumbling computer nerd' who hacked into the government computers to prove that the United States government was covering up evidence of Unidentified Flying Objects (UFOs). Supporters of McKinnon believe that his hacking has revealed important weaknesses in the United States government's computer systems, that must be made more secure. McKinnon faces up to 70 years in prison if he is sent to the United States to stand trial.

Gary McKinnon allegedly hacked into some of the world's most classified material. He claims he did not mean to cause harm; others say his actions were malicious.

Viruses, worms and Trojan horses

When you turn on your computer and open an email or start a game, you expect to be able to read the email or play the game. But if your computer screen suddenly turns into a whirl of numbers, symbols and shapes which have no relation to what you press on the keyboard, it probably means that a virus has attacked your computer. A virus doesn't mean your computer has broken down because of a fault in the computer. The virus is a specially designed program, created by someone else to damage your software.

Malware (the word is made from 'malicious and software') describes deliberately harmful software which includes viruses, worms and Trojan horses. The virus spreads to other programs on the computer it has infected. A worm does the same damage, but it also spreads copies of itself to other computers, often through computer networks. Trojan horses look as if they are free programs, such as games, but they are in fact ways to harm your software.

A hacker can gain remote access to your webcam and can therefore spy on you as you use it.

How do hackers use Trojan horses?

You might be on a great website and want to download some freeware to play a new game, but instead you unknowingly download a Trojan horse, an unwanted software that 'spies' on your computer. This 'spyware' acts as a door through which a hacker can access information on your computer and remotely control your computer. Hackers can access information, change programs, or perform other functions on a computer without the computer user knowing anything about it. A hacker, once he or she has gained access to your computer, can do whatever you do on your computer. This includes deleting, renaming and changing files, sending emails and even viewing your webcam.

Why create viruses, worms and Trojan horses?

Some people create malware simply to cause disruption to individuals and organizations. It's a bit like vandalizing a car – pointless and malicious. Others do it to get hold of private information, which they then use for criminal purposes. For example, a Trojan horse can give a hacker access to someone's credit card details and financial information. They can use this information to steal money from someone's bank account.

In the media

In 2000, many thousands of unsuspecting computer users opened up emails with ILOVEYOU in the subject heading. But this was no innocent declaration of love. It was a computer virus that infected every computer running Microsoft Windows that it reached. It spread quickly, sending itself to all the contacts on a user's computer. It infected about 10% of the world's computers, causing billions of pounds worth of damage to businesses and individuals. Even the seat of the British government in London, the House of Commons, had to shut down its email system for a while.

Police in the Philippines suspected several people of spreading the virus. However, they were unable to take any action against them because at that time in the Philippines there was no law against writing viruses.

11

Spam

Spam is unsolicited commercial or bulk email. Basically, it's emails from people you don't know, which you didn't ask for and probably don't want. Spammers (people who send spam) get email addresses from scanning programs such as Usenet and mailing lists. According to some estimates, spam makes up 80% of email traffic! The messages are sometimes advertisements that clog up a person's inbox and which take time to delete. But sometimes the spam is unpleasant and upsetting. Some spam takes the form of an email chain letter which says you will have bad luck if you break the chain and don't forward the email. This is totally untrue and the only purpose of the chain email is to send out more viruses and more spam. Delete them!

Every day, hundreds of billions of spam emails clog up inboxes around the world.

In the media

In 2008, two spammers, Sanford Wallace and Walter Rines, were found guilty of spamming thousands of messages to users on the MySpace website. They were eventually caught and fined $230 million (£118 million). Wallace and Rines sent more than 700,000 messages to MySpace users. The messages tricked the users into visiting gambling sites or adult pages. There were notes on these pages that looked as if they were from the user's friends. In fact, the notes contained advertisements and whenever a user clicked on the note, the advertisers paid money to the spammers. Hemanshu Nigam, chief security officer for MySpace, maintains that MySpace operates a policy of zero tolerance towards people who act illegally on the site and that the organization is committed to tracking down and punishing offenders.

Is spam illegal?

Sending emails isn't against the law. However, in many countries it is against the law to use personal information without permission. Some spammers have been found guilty of using personal information on databases to send spam emails. Several people have been found guilty of sending pornographic material in spam messages. In the United States, the Can-Spam Act (Controlling the Assault of Non-Solicited Pornography and Marketing) means that spammers can be taken to court over spam. However, the reality is that even if one spammer is stopped, there are many more who will continue.

Always check an email is genuine before confirming any personal details.

Trick spams

Phishing is sending a spam email asking for confirmation of bank details. The emails look genuine, and often use the logos and symbols of the real bank. The email asks the computer user to click on a website link. The user is then asked to confirm lots of personal information, including details about bank or savings accounts. The phisher uses these details to steal money, and sometimes even a person's identity. They might open up new bank accounts in the victim's name and use their money.

13

Criminal networks

Many hackers work alone. Others work in highly organized criminal gangs, using sophisticated techniques to produce malware. The writers or creators of the malware can remotely control a network of computers around the world, all infected with the malware and spread it to other computers. This network is called a botnet.

Megacrash

Sometimes, an individual, or a group, targets a well-known website or service such as Amazon or the search engine Google. Then, all at the same time, they send vast amounts of information or requests for information to the site. The site is overloaded and cannot deal with genuine queries, and is forced to become unavailable. This deliberate targeting is called denial of service, and it is against the law.

In 2000, cyberattacks against sites such as eBay and Yahoo were so severe that the then president of the United States, Bill Clinton, called a summit to discuss how to combat computer hacking.

In the
media

Shadowcrew was a huge network of criminals involved in identity theft. The gang used phishing and Trojan horse viruses to collect details of people's bank accounts, addresses and passwords. This was all the information they needed to apply for more credit cards, withdraw money and buy goods using someone else's identity. The criminals were stealing millions of pounds. After a year-long operation begun in 2003 and run by the United States Secret Service, in 2004, the police arrested 28 people in seven different countries.

Nigerian email scam

Two Nigerians living in London were found guilty of the so-called Nigerian letter scam and were sent to prison for over a year. In this fraud, innocent people received emails which appeared to come from the Nigerian government. The emails promised lots of money in return for putting funds in a bank account. They looked genuine, so many people were tricked into parting with their cash.

Invisible auction

You or your parents or carers may have bought or sold goods on the online auction site, eBay. When you buy on an online auction site, you are buying goods you can't see. Most people sell and buy goods in this way successfully, but some people use the anonymity of the Internet to cheat and trick others out of their money. They receive the money for goods, but never actually send them. The police work alongside eBay to try to catch the criminals when this happens, but if you use auction sites check you are dealing with a genuine seller or buyer and don't send cash in the post.

Stealing

Some people may use the Internet to steal and make money. This is becoming increasingly common as people use the Internet to shop. When you shop online, you hand over your bank or credit card details and these are stored on the computer. If a hacker has used a Trojan horse to get into your computer, or has hacked into the seller's website, your details are there for all to see. Some criminals make huge amounts of money by selling on these personal details to other criminals. According to the Organization for Security and Cooperation in Europe, criminals steal an estimated $100 billion a year from computer users.

Criminals hack into bank accounts and empty them of all money – leaving the victim with nothing when they go to the cash machine.

It happened to me

'Last year, I got a great offer by email to buy some CDs really cheaply. I told Mum and she said I could buy them. She used her credit card to buy the CDs for me – but the CDs never turned up. Instead, over £500 was taken from Mum's account. She was so shocked – we will never fall for something like that again.'

Ben, aged 12.

TALK ABOUT

* Do you think there is ever a situation when there is a valid reason for hacking?
* How do you think online fraud can upset and harm someone, or do you think it is harmless because there is no physical contact?

Identity theft

Criminals search the Internet for personal information, such as an individual's date of birth or address. With this information, they can apply for credit cards or set up new bank accounts. They often spend huge amounts of money that does not belong to them. In the United Kingdom in 2006, more than £212 million was spent by criminals using credit cards illegally online or over the telephone.

If you are shopping online, you probably need to give your name and address, but be careful about sharing personal information on any websites.

Chapter 3

Illegal material on the Internet

The Internet has revolutionized the way we find and share information. In seconds, you can communicate with someone on the other side of the world. You can surf the Internet and discover interesting websites and useful sources of information for school projects. But you can also come across unpleasant and sometimes illegal content.

Crime via the Internet

Some people take advantage of the ease with which the Internet links millions of users around the world, and use it for harmful and criminal purposes. Such activity ranges from encouraging violent behaviour to coordinating terrorist activities.

Terrorist organizations increasingly use the Internet to communicate, spread their propaganda and recruit new members.

Why do terrorists use the Internet?

Terrorists use the Internet for several reasons. It crosses countries and borders, it is fast, it can be anonymous, it can reach huge numbers of people and, if necessary, a website can quickly be removed. Terrorists use the Internet to attract new members to their cause, spread information, raise money and find out information about their enemies and targets. They also use it to set up and arrange terrorist attacks.

In parts of India, where terrorists are known to have organized attacks from cybercafés, the owners of the cafés must record details of any Internet user and hand them to police if necessary.

The terrorist attacks in the United States on 11 September 2001 were partly planned by members of the Al-Qaeda terrorist group using the Internet. After the attacks, police found many coded messages on one of the terrorists' computers. The terrorists had communicated via chatrooms and email using cybercafés or computers in public places, making it harder to trace the user.

In the media

In Scotland in 2007, a young man called Mohammed Atif Siddique was found guilty of terrorism offences, based largely upon material found on his laptop and on websites he had visited. Siddique's lawyer unsuccessfully argued that researching and looking at terrorist websites did not necessarily mean the computer user was an active terrorist.

Racism

In 1999, the National Criminal Intelligence Service in the United Kingdom first identified that the Internet was being used to spread racism. In the United Kingdom spreading racist material is illegal.

If you come across a website which you believe spreads racism, you should contact the hosting ISP and make a complaint. ISPs have their own guidelines for what is acceptable content. If the content of the website does not fit in with their guidelines, they can remove it.

When is it against the law?

In the United Kingdom it is against the law to stir up racial hatred against a group of people defined by their colour, race, nationality or ethnic origin. This includes material on the Internet. In the United States, hate groups, racist websites and other racist publications contradict the ideals of the country, but they are not punishable by law. This means that it is not possible for the British police to prosecute someone in the United States who spreads racist material on the Internet, even though it can be viewed in the United Kingdom.

In the United Kingdom in 1998, one government minister, Jack Straw, was concerned about material on the Internet which denied the mass killing of Jews during the Second World War, known as the Holocaust. However, he was worried about creating a law that would make this illegal because it might deny people's basic freedom to express their opinions. He was also concerned that introducing such legislation would play into the hands of people who deny the Holocaust and draw more attention to the material they publish. Currently, it is not illegal in the United Kingdom to deny the Holocaust, although it is illegal in other countries.

Millions of Jews were killed in concentration camps during the Holocaust. Some websites deny that this atrocity ever took place.

TALK ABOUT

✱ Do you think people should be allowed to publish whatever they want on the Internet, in order to protect freedom of speech, or should there be strict laws on what is allowed?

Adult sites

Have you ever been on the Internet and come across some upsetting sexual images or images of violence? It can be distressing, confusing and frightening. It's important you know what to do if this happens and to remember that you haven't done anything wrong. Even if you weren't meant to be surfing at the time, it's far more important to tell your parents or carers what you have come across than to keep it to yourself.

Some images are illegal and others are not, but they can be shocking and upsetting. It is illegal to send sexual pictures, called pornography, to a child, but when spam is sent, which often includes such inappropriate material, the spammer has no idea of the age of the person receiving the spam.

There are special software filters that can block young people coming across pornography when they browse the Internet. However, these filters also restrict genuine searches. For instance, a young person might be blocked from visiting a site that offers useful information about the facts on growing up and sexual health.

FACTS

✳ **The Internet pornography industry makes about $12 billion dollars a year.**

✳ **Approximately 20% of all Internet pornography involves children.**

Tell your parents or carers about any frightening and shocking sites, or any inappropriate spam that you come across.

It's only pictures

Young people are usually more skilled in using computers than their parents or carers. If a young person is better able to navigate the Internet, to download, upload and sort out connection problems then, some might argue, why can't they see whatever they want on the Internet? Yet, others say young people's minds and feelings are still developing. They are more at risk from the negative effects of offensive images and ideas than adults.

Young people are curious and may have deliberately tried to bypass any filtering software installed on the computer. They then may come across sites that are upsetting. In this situation, tell your parents or carers, even if you know you shouldn't have been using the Internet in this way. It's much better to let your parents know what you have seen rather than to keep it a secret and feel frightened and upset.

Harmful sites

Some websites encourage vulnerable people to harm themselves. This is not necessarily illegal but can be very dangerous. You may have heard of sites that encourage young people suffering from anorexia nervosa to continue their eating disorder. These sites even provide tips and ideas to help sufferers lose more weight. If you come across such a site, or any other sites that encourage harmful behaviour, tell your parents or carers. It's important to realize that the people who post information and so-called advice on these sites do so without a care for you or your wellbeing.

Certain websites encourage vulnerable people to starve themselves. Always tell an adult you trust if you come across such a site.

23

Violence

Some research shows that if children and young people see lots of images of violence, or play very aggressive online games, they can become numb to the real effects of violence. This can lead to aggressive and abusive behaviour in real life.

About six hours of video footage is uploaded onto the website YouTube every minute. This makes it impractical for YouTube to monitor and check every video that is shown. However, YouTube has guidelines about what is acceptable on the site. Images encouraging or glorifying violence are not allowed.

Age guidance

Most people would agree that it is not right for a child to see a film with an 18 rating. Some people think websites should also have age ratings as this will help young people and parents to search the Internet more confidently and safely. Others argue that the system would be impossible to enforce because there are so many sites and not all would agree to stick to the rating system.

Even if you are not meant to be on a certain game or site, tell your parents or carers if you come across extremely violent or shocking images.

If you know that a game or site is not suitable for your age, think about it before you use it. It is unsuitable for a reason and this is usually to protect you. It's important to take responsibility for your own safety and wellbeing.

Films and computer or video games have age guidelines. There is much discussion about how practical similar age guidelines on websites might be.

DOs & DON'Ts

✳ Do make sure your Internet searches contain several relevant words rather than just one. This makes it less likely that the search will bring up unsuitable websites.

✳ Do ask your parents or carers to complain to the search engine or your ISP provider if you come across unsuitable material.

✳ Do complain to the United Kingdom's Internet Watch Foundation (IWF) if you come across what you think is illegal material (www.iwf.org.uk).

✳ Do be suspicious of any website that asks you not to tell your parents or carers you have been on it. The only exception to this is where young people are in danger from their own parents or carers.

✳ Do tell your parents or carers if you receive spam that contains sexual images.

✳ Don't try to bypass any firewalls or security settings your parents or carers have put in place.

Chapter 4

How chatting online can become a crime

On social networking websites such as MySpace, Bebo and Facebook you can chat with friends online and make new friends who share your hobbies and interests. You can meet people online, chat, share photos and even videos online. However, it can also be dangerous, and it's important to know how to protect yourself when communicating with people you haven't met.

Personal information

It's easy to feel confident chatting to someone via a computer screen. This confidence can potentially lead to difficult situations, such as you giving away too much personal information. Even though you know you shouldn't give out personal details, some people are skilled at making you feel relaxed, so you may feel happy mentioning where your school is or where you hang out so they can find you. It's most likely these people don't want genuine friendships.

Dangers

You may use the Internet for fun, but you cannot guarantee that everyone else who has access to your chats and photos has such innocent intentions. It's great fun sharing photos of yourself and friends, and having a laugh, but think carefully before you do it. Are you wearing a school uniform? If you are, a person with harmful intentions could find out which school you go to and follow you there.

Chatting online can seem like harmless fun, but the intentions of the person you are speaking to may be questionable.

The law

Some countries, including the United Kingdom and Australia, have laws which mean a person can be arrested for befriending a child if they intend to cause harm. The police can arrest them before any harm comes to the child. In Australia in 2007, a man using the name Hinkley spent more than six months chatting on the Internet to an 11-year-old girl. During the course of the Internet chat, it became clear that the man's intentions were harmful. In this case the 'girl' to whom Hinkley was chatting was actually an undercover police officer. Hinkley was arrested before he could harm anyone else.

You may think you are chatting to a teenage boy (you might even see photographs of him on your computer), but the reality is you may be chatting to an older man.

TALK ABOUT

* Have you ever felt uncomfortable in an online chatroom?
* What would you do if you felt suspicious about someone's intentions, or if you thought you had given out too much personal information?

Grooming

A few people use the Internet with harmful intentions. They carefully build up relationships with children and young people. They then try to meet them for sexual reasons. This is called grooming. Some people go to considerable efforts to pretend to be someone else online, so they can meet young people. They might make fake names and webcam images so they seem younger than they really are. For instance, a 50-year-old man could pretend to be a teenager.

In 2007, a massive police operation broke up an international criminal ring of adults who harmed children. These people are called paedophiles. The suspects used an Internet chatroom to swap images of children and young people being sexually abused. More than 30 children may have been saved from harm as a result of the police operation. Philip Thompson, the man who ran the criminal ring, was arrested and sent to prison indefinitely.

In the media

In January 2009, a fifteen-year-old girl from the United Kingdom called Laura Stainforth told her parents she was going shopping, but did not return home. Her disappearance sparked a huge police hunt and she was spotted in France with a man who police believe she had met on the Internet, six months earlier. The man was already under investigation by the police for harming another girl he had met online. The police arrested the man and returned Laura to her family. The man is currently awaiting trial.

Child abusers often spend months befriending young people and gaining their trust. They may then send them pornographic material, ask them to meet or blackmail them into doing something they don't want to do.

DOs & DON'Ts

✳ Don't give away too much information about yourself (phone numbers, school, real name, address, email address), however long you have been chatting to someone.

✳ Do be aware that in chatrooms other people can see what you are writing, and they might use the information to find you.

✳ Don't keep an online relationship a secret, even if the other person wants you to. Ask yourself what the other person is hiding.

✳ Don't meet people you chat to over the Internet. If you decide you really must, only do it if your parent(s) or carer, goes with you, and make sure you meet in a public place.

✳ Don't send anyone pictures of yourself.

✳ Do tell your parents or carers if you meet someone who you think is pretending to be someone else, or who begins to send you messages that make you feel uncomfortable in any way.

Never go alone to meet someone you have only 'met' online. You are placing yourself at risk.

Chapter 5

Is bullying on the Internet a crime?

Bullying can take the form of teasing, deliberately excluding or leaving someone out and spreading rumours. This can happen in the real world, and the virtual world. Cyberbullying is bullying via the Internet. It doesn't cause direct physical harm, but it can cause huge distress and unhappiness.

Bullying online

Just like face-to-face bullying, cyberbullying is unpleasant, cruel and wrong. Although it is not always a crime in itself, if the bully commits a crime such as destroying material on a person's computer, or making threats, then it is illegal. Laws about cyberbullying vary from country to country.

A wide audience

You don't need a computer to access the Internet. Many mobile phones can get access to the Internet. As a result, some schools have banned the use of mobile phones at school. This is partly because the phones can distract pupils from their studies, and partly because they can be used in cyberbullying.

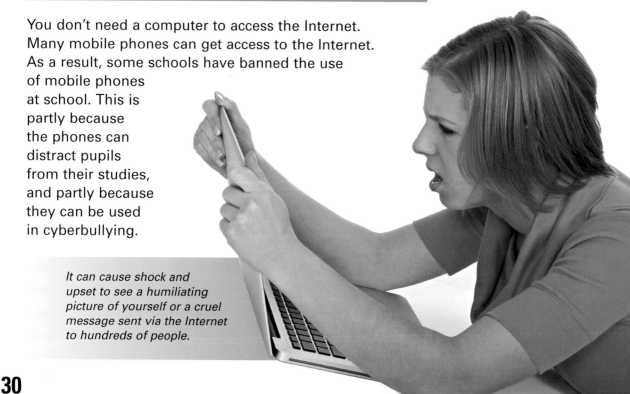

It can cause shock and upset to see a humiliating picture of yourself or a cruel message sent via the Internet to hundreds of people.

It is very frightening to be pursued by bullying messages online.

Hiding behind the Internet

At the click of a button, a cyberbully can spread a nasty message or a threat to lots of people. Cyberbullies often feel protected by technology – they think that using a computer or mobile phone protects their identity. This gives them more confidence, and their behaviour may be nastier and bolder. Although emails and text messages are hard to trace, it is possible to find out where they come from.

In the
media

In a small city called Dardenne Prairie, in the American state of Missouri, a 13-year-old girl called Megan Meier killed herself. Megan had been the victim of a long campaign of bullying and hate on MySpace. At first, it was thought the bullying was from a MySpace profile belonging to a boy called Josh Evans. However, Megan's parents discovered that the Josh Evans profile was false. The bullies were actually a girl with whom Megan had fallen out and that girl's mother. The mother was found guilty of unauthorized access to a computer system with intent to harm another person. As a result of Megan's death, Dardenne Prairie introduced a local law making any form of online harassment a crime for which a person would have to pay a fine or face imprisonment.

Phone attacks

In some parts of the world, there have been incidents of people using their mobile phones to film attacks on individuals. These attacks are known as 'happy slapping', but the activity is far from happy. An innocent victim is attacked and the attack is filmed on a mobile phone. The film is sent out to mobile phones and posted on the Internet and victims can be seriously hurt, even killed. Happy slapping is against the law and both the attackers and the person filming the attack can be taken to court and sentenced.

If you receive an image like this on your mobile or the Internet, don't send it on. Think about how the victim feels. If you are the victim of a happy slapping incident, don't feel ashamed; first tell an adult you trust. If the bullying continues, you can report the abuse to an anti-bullying organization (see page 47), to your ISP or to the police. Message boards carrying threats, abuse and false messages can be shut down. Sometimes, it is possible for the police to trace the source of such messages. Happy slappers and cyberbullies must be stopped before they attack someone else.

It is terrifying to feel that someone is constantly watching you.

TALK ABOUT

✴ **How would you define cyberbullying?**

✴ **When do you think cyberbullying crosses the line from being just nasty and becomes a crime?**

Cyberstalking

Cyberstalking is when someone keeps pestering an individual online, with unwanted messages and threats. It can happen to children and adults. You may wonder how it can be harmful to be 'stalked' or followed on the Internet. After all, no one is physically following you or watching you, but imagine how it feels to have someone following you online. Whenever you turn on the computer or your phone, there's a message from someone you don't know or don't want to be in contact with. They have found out your email address and other details. In many countries this harassing behaviour is also illegal. Tell a trusted adult if you are the victim of cyberstalking.

Chapter 6

Music, films and games

You might share photos, jokes and chat on the Internet. Do you also share music files with friends, or download copies of films? If you do, and you haven't obtained the necessary permission, you could be breaking the law to do with copyright.

What is copyright?

If you write a song, or record your song with some friends, you own the copyright to that song. That means that you have the legal right to copy it and make money from the copyright of your music. Other people cannot use it, unless you give them permission or they have paid you an agreed amount to do so.

P2P

Peer-to-Peer (P2P) is a popular way of sharing files. It allows file sharing, or swapping music or other files, on P2P networks. It links one user to millions of others. Instead of downloading from a website, a P2P user is downloading music from another user. Downloading P2P software allows you to share lots of files. But there are some illegal uses of P2P networks which many people are unaware of.

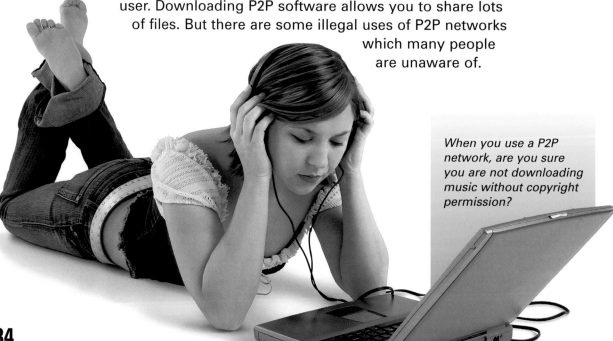

When you use a P2P network, are you sure you are not downloading music without copyright permission?

One study showed that teenagers have more than 800 illegally copied songs on their digital music players.

Music matters

MP3 is a digital music format which allows the user to make music tracks smaller. MP3 files can be played on a computer using special programs. They make it easy to download music over the Internet. The popularity of MP3s has led to a rise in music piracy, especially through file sharing programs such as P2P. Some websites which offered MP3 music files for free to download were sued for breaking copyright. Some record companies put special software on their music CDs to make it more difficult for people to copy them onto their computer.

Musicians make most of their money from the copyright of their music. If you make a copy of someone else's music without permission, you are breaking the law. You could have to pay a fine if you are caught.

FACTS

According to one survey of children in the United States aged 11–14:

✳ About 8 million people around the world are using a file sharing network at any one time.

✳ There are more than 900 million illegal music files available for download on a number of file sharing networks.

✳ File sharing was the most used service on the Internet in 2008.

Lots of laws

The laws concerning copyright and the Internet are complicated, and they vary around the world. For example, in Canada downloading copyright music from P2P networks is legal, but uploading those files is not. In the United States, it is illegal to copy copyrighted music, unless the copy is for your own use only. Illegal use of copyrighted music can be punished by a prison sentence of three years and a hefty fine.

Is what you are doing within the law?

If you upload a song from a CD to a P2P network you are technically breaking the law because you are helping other users of the network to make illegal copies. Even if you don't know they are doing it, you could be held responsible for this.

It breaks copyright law to copy a song or film from a social messaging site such as Facebook or Bebo, or to send it to contacts on your list or use the music unless you have permission to do so. Sharing copyrighted music, games, films and software, unless you have permission or you have paid to copy it, is against the law.

If you download music or films onto your parent or carer's computer without copyright permission. They may have to pay a fine or even have access to their ISP cut off.

However, it is legal to download songs that have been put on the Internet with the permission of the record company and recording artist from approved sites such as Apple iTunes and Napster. You usually have to pay to download from these sites.

A victimless crime?

Some people think that downloading material from the Internet without permission doesn't matter. No one gets hurt. You aren't taking money from someone's wallet. Others argue that the people who work in the music industry suffer. If people don't pay for CDs, there is less money to pay all the people who work towards producing the music, from the sound engineers to the singers.

ISPs, which provide access to the Internet, are getting tough on piracy. They can send out warning letters to people who download illegally. If the person continues to download illegally, the ISP may even cut off their Internet access.

Artists lose out if they do not receive royalties for their work.

A genuine file or a virus?

P2P files are not always what they seem. You may think you are swapping a music file or a game, but you may also be getting a virus. Sometimes you may receive a file that is not what you expected, and that contains unpleasant and unwelcome content. It is illegal to knowingly spread a computer virus.

A malware designed to steal passwords and usernames from players of online games once made its way into space! A laptop on the International Space Station (ISS) was infected with a virus. The safe and successful operation of the Space Station, which orbits Earth, depends on a complex network of computers. Antivirus software detected the virus. NASA spokespeople said that there was no risk to any of NASA's computer systems because the virus was detected and the laptop was not linked to those used to run the space station. However, if a virus had interfered with the running of the space station, the effects would have been devastating.

High above Earth in space, astronauts on board the ISS were using laptops infected with a virus.

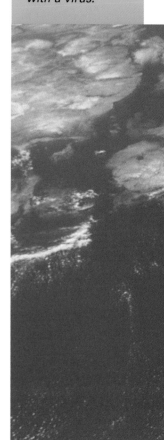

DOs & DON'Ts

* Do choose a username that doesn't give away any personal information.

* Don't give away your email address or any personal information when online.

* Do ask your parents or carers before downloading any software you need.

* Do tell your parents or carers if you feel uncomfortable about what is happening on a website or in a game, or if another player upsets you.

Online games

It's great to go online and play a game with several other players, from an adventure game to a card game. You don't need to be round at a friend's house or have a friend at yours – although that's fun, too. Online games also have hidden dangers, just like any other online connection that links lots of people. You might be linking up to people you don't know. By sharing your computer network, you can download programs that might not be genuine, or may contain a virus that is then used to 'spy' on your computer and passwords. There is the danger in giving away personal information, such as an email address or your real name, that someone with harmful intentions could use the information against you.

TALK ABOUT

* Even though it's against the law, do you think it's OK to download and share music files, because all your friends do it?

* Why do you think there are laws about copyright, and do you think these are fair?

* Do the risks about online games make you more cautious, or do you think the dangers are unlikely to affect you?

Chapter 7

What can we do to stop Internet crime?

As long as the Internet is working, there will be Internet crime. Criminals will find new ways of tricking, cheating and stealing online. Hackers will devise more complex codes to bypass firewalls and antivirus software. We can't stop cybercrime, but we can help prevent ourselves becoming victims of it.

Being aware

As the police and authorities try to catch up with the pace and scope of Internet crime, public awareness of the dangers is increasing. Individuals are responsible for protecting their own computer systems and personal information. There is a lot of unpleasant material on the Internet, but it's not always illegal and it's not always possible to stop it. This makes it important for every Internet user to be aware of the risks of unsuitable material, and to protect themselves.

It's safer to use the Internet in a family room where you are less likely to feel threatened or pressurized into sharing personal details.

Protection

A firewall prevents access to your computer from other computers. It's like a safety net around your computer. Firewalls can stop Trojan horses and other malware from communicating with and infecting your computer.

Preventing computer crime is a family business. If you share a computer with your parents or carers and brothers and sisters, you all need to follow the same guidelines, otherwise your computer is at risk.

Firewalls prevent you accessing inappropriate material.

DOs & DON'Ts

✳ **Don't reply to spam. Doing so just confirms your email address and results in lots more spam.**

✳ **Don't click on 'unsubscribe' to spam – it only confirms your email address and results in more spam.**

✳ **Don't buy anything from a spammer – this too encourages more spam.**

✳ **Do set up your email account so that your email or webmail program can block and then separate what it thinks is spam, or junk mail.**

✳ **Do make sure your parents or carers instal a firewall on all computers.**

✳ **Don't download free antivirus software – it may contain a Trojan horse.**

Police and cybercrime

Many countries have special police forces to deal with cybercrime. The global nature of the Internet makes policing it very difficult. The police in one country don't necessarily have the power to take action over illegal online activity if the activity began in a different country. However, to stop criminals from using the Internet to harm children, there are international efforts from many police forces to catch criminals.

If criminals use websites to boast about their crimes or taunt their enemies, the police, too, can use the Internet to catch criminals and prevent crime. In some cities in the United States, the police watch sites such as MySpace so they can identify members of illegal gangs from postings on the sites.

Sites such as MySpace reach huge numbers of people. This means they can be useful tools for the police to communicate with the public. In some cases, they can use the sites to appeal for witnesses to help them catch criminals. In the United Kingdom, the police ran a campaign on the social networking site Bebo to show young people the dangers and risks of carrying knives.

These forensic scientists are examining data on a computer for evidence of Internet crimes.

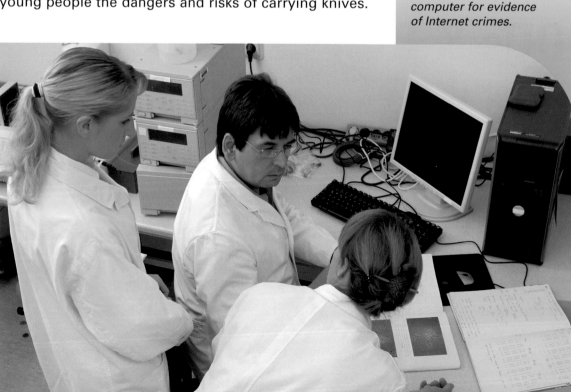

The role of ISPs

Today, ISPs are taking an active role in preventing criminal activity carried out through their servers. They work with the police and other organizations to make sure that sites which show illegal material, or are used for criminal purposes, are taken down.

It is important to protect online users from crime, but people argue that it is as important to protect freedom of speech. For instance, in China during the 2008 Olympic Games, the Chinese authorities blocked many websites. This prevented Chinese people from accessing information that was accessible (and legal) to people elsewhere around the world, such as the United States.

Face of the future

Companies spend a lot of money protecting their computers. In an attempt to stay ahead of the criminals, some companies may start to use 'biometrics'. This uses a person's bodily features for identification. Biometric technology can 'read' a computer user's eyes, identify their voice and check their fingerprints. This would make it a lot more difficult for someone to pretend to be someone else, even with access to their password.

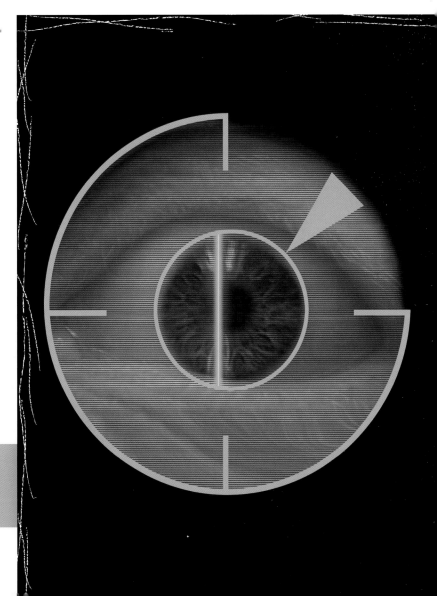

A biometric scan reads the user's eyes to check his or her identity.

Digital footprint

Think before you post, forward or send any material on the Internet. Do you know who is going to see what you are sending? Would you be embarrassed if your parents or other people saw it?

Many people think that they are anonymous behind their computer – but every time you register for a new website or upload photos, you leave behind a trail of your computer activity, called a digital footprint. Criminals use personal details to steal money or buy goods in your name. Be aware, too, that universities and employers sometimes look at the profiles of prospective students or employees on sites such as Facebook. What might seem fun and a bit of a laugh when a person is in their teens might turn out to be a serious embarrassment later in life.

Spending time on the Internet is brilliant for research, fun and socializing, but it's important to balance being online with having fun with friends.

Computer time

It's not a crime to spend lots of time on the computer, but it can become a bit of an obsession. Keep computer use fun by spending time doing other things with friends as well. Be aware of the risks from other computer users to stay safe online.

TALK ABOUT

* Do you know anyone who has used the Internet in an illegal way? What should you do if you find someone has used the Internet illegally?

* Do you think you have ever been a victim of Internet crime?

DOs & DON'Ts

* Do follow your parents' or carers' guidelines about which sites you can access.

* Do tell your parents about the possible dangers on the Internet.

* Don't delete evidence of cyberbullying – if the police become involved, they will need to see it.

* Do ask parents or carers for permission to use credit card details.

* Don't give away personal information.

* Do check that a padlock icon appears at the bottom of your browser window, or the web address begins with https: if you buy goods over the Internet. This shows that the site is secure.

* Don't follow links in an email which ask you to confirm personal information.

* Do think carefully before adding someone to your list of online friends.

* Do remember that people are not always who they say they are online. Never arrange to meet someone you have met online. If you decide that you must, then tell your parents or carers and make sure you go with a responsible adult who can protect you if necessary.

Glossary

anonymous To do something without giving away your true identity.

biometric A form of technology that identifies people through bodily characteristics, such as eyes and voice patterns.

botnet A network of computers that are programmed to send viruses to other computers.

classified Confidential.

copyright The rights over material, such as a song, which belong to the person who created the material.

crime An act which breaks the law.

download To transfer information from the Internet onto your computer.

email A way of sending messages and information across the Internet using languages such as smtp.

firewall Hardware or software to protect computers from viruses.

fraud An illegal act by which someone pretends to be something or someone they are not.

grooming Getting to know a child or young person, with harmful intentions.

Internet A network that connects millions of computers worldwide.

ISP An Internet service provider is a company that provides access to the Internet.

malware A computer program that is designed to alter other computer hardware and software.

paedophile A person who is sexually attracted to children or young people.

personal identity Important information about a person such as their name and bank account.

piracy To illegally copy or download copyrighted material.

pornography Sexually explicit material.

propaganda Persuasive information a person or an organization releases to the public.

royalties Monies that an artist, such as a writer or musician, receives from the sale of their work.

software A coded computer program or instruction.

software filter A system that can be loaded onto a computer. The filter will block any unsuitable material on the Internet.

spam Unsolicited commercial or bulk email.

terrorist A person who uses terror and violence to promote their cause.

vandalize To damage or destroy deliberately.

Further information

Notes for Teachers:
The Talk About panels are to be used to encourage debate and avoid the polarization of views. One way of doing this is to use 'continuum lines'. Think of a range of statements or opinions about the topics that can then be considered by the pupils. An imaginary line is constructed that pupils can stand along to show what they feel in response to each statement (please see above). If they strongly agree or disagree with the viewpoint they can stand by the signs, if the response is somewhere in between they stand along the line in the relevant place. If the response is 'neither agree, nor disagree' or they 'don't know' then they stand at an equal distance from each sign, in the middle. Alternatively, continuum lines can be drawn out on paper and pupils can mark a cross on the line to reflect their views.

Books to read

The Internet and Worldwide Web (Getting the Message) by Sean Connolly (Franklin Watts, 2009)

Personal Safety (Know the Facts) by Judith Anderson (Wayland, 2009)

Websites and helplines

Internet Watch Foundation
A site run by the Internet Watch Foundation (IWF) which you can contact if you come across what you think is illegal material.
Website: http://www.iwf.org.uk

The BBC website
A useful site with plenty of advice on Internet safety.
Website:
http://www.bbc.co.uk/chatguide/antisocial/grooming.shtml

BullyingUK
This site has lots of advice about cyberbullying, and you can report some instances of cyberbullying here.
Website:
http://www.bullying.co.uk

ThinkUKnow
A great site with lots of tips for people of all ages about safety and technology.
Website:
http://www.thinkuknow.co.uk

Childnet International
This website is designed for parents, young people and teachers to advise them on ways to stay safe.
Website:
http://www.childnet.com/kia

The NSPCC
This website is run by the NSPCC (United Kingdom) to support young people facing difficult issues, such as bullying or abuse.
Website:
http://www.there4me.com/home/index.asp

The United Kingdom government site
This United Kingdom government site has advice on dealing with cyberbullying.
Website:
http://www.direct.gov.uk/en/YoungPeople/HealthAnd Relationships/Bullying/DG_070502

Index

Entries in **bold** are for pictures.

TALK ABOUT

WAYLAND

Contents of titles in the series:

Bullying

978 0 7502 4617 0
1. Let's talk about bullying
2. What is bullying?
3. How does it feel to be bullied?
4. Who gets bullied?
5. Why do people bully?
6. Beating bullying
7. Bullying in society

Eating Disorders and Body Image

978 0 7502 4936 2
1. What are eating disorders?
2. Food and the body
3. What does it mean to have an eating disorder?
4. Who gets eating disorders?
5. What causes eating disorders?
6. Preventing problems
7. The treatment of eating disorders

Gangs and Knife Crime

978 0 7502 5735 0
1. What are gang and knife crime?
2. Different kinds of gang
3. What do gangs do?
4. Why do people get involved in gangs and knife crime?
5. The effects of gang and knife crime
6. What does the law say?
7. Can we stop gangs and knife crime?
8. Staying safe

Internet Crime

978 0 7502 5736 7
1. What is Internet crime?
2. Spying, stealing and vandalizing
3. Illegal material on the Internet
4. How chatting online can become a crime
5. Is bullying on the Internet a crime?
6. Music, films and games
7. What can we do to stop Internet crime?

Sex and Puberty

978 0 7502 5738 1
1. What is puberty?
2. What happens to girls during puberty?
3. What happens to boys during puberty?
4. What are sexual feelings?
5. What is safe sex?
6. What emotions do you feel during puberty?
7. Relationships
8. Dealing with the changes

Drugs

978 0 7502 4937 9
1. What are drugs?
2. Why do we take drugs?
3. What about drinking and smoking?
4. What's the law on drugs?
5. What about cannabis?
6. What other drugs are there?
7. Paying the price
8. It's your choice

Family Break-Ups

978 0 7502 4934 8
1. What is family break-up?
2. Why do families break up?
3. How do people feel in a family break-up?
4. What happens when a family breaks up?
5. People's attitudes to family break-up
6. The law and family break-up
7. What challenges does the 'new' family face?
8. Moving on

Homelessness

978 0 7502 5737 4
1. What is homelessness?
2. Why do people become homeless?
3. Homelessness and children
4. Addiction and homelessness
5. Staying clean and healthy
6. Mental health
7. Working and earning
8. Helping the homeless

Racism

978 0 7502 4935 5
1. What is racism?
2. Why are people racist?
3. What do racists do?
4. Hidden racism
5. What is religious prejudice?
6. Racism against migrants
7. Nazi racial policies
8. What can we do about racism?

Youth Crime

978 0 7502 4938 6
1. What is crime?
2. Crime past and present
3. Why does youth crime happen?
4. Behaving badly
5. Crimes of theft
6. Crimes of violence
7. What happens if you commit a crime?
8. What can you do about crime?